Reading Comprehension

Written by **Shannon Keeley**

Illustrations by **Chris Murphy**

FlashKids

An imprint of Sterling Children's Books

This book belongs to

_____

FLASH KIDS, STERLING, and the distinctive Sterling logo are registered trademarks of
Sterling Publishing Co., Inc.

Published by Sterling Publishing Co., Inc.
387 Park Avenue South, New York, NY 10016
Text and illustrations © 2007 by Flash Kids
Distributed in Canada by Sterling Publishing
c/o Canadian Manda Group, 165 Dufferin Street
Toronto, Ontario, Canada M6K 3H6
Distributed in the United Kingdom by GMC Distribution Services
Castle Place, 166 High Street, Lewes, East Sussex, England BN7 1XU
Distributed in Australia by Capricorn Link (Australia) Pty. Ltd.
P.O. Box 704, Windsor, NSW 2756, Australia

Sterling ISBN 978-1-4114-3477-6

Manufactured in China

Lot #:
4 6 8 10 9 7 5
10/12

For information about custom editions, special sales, premium and
corporate purchases, please contact Sterling Special Sales
Department at 800-805-5489 or specialsales@sterlingpublishing.com.

Cover design and production by Mada Design, Inc.

Dear Parent,

Once young children have learned to read, the next important step is to ensure that they understand and retain the information they encounter. The passages and activities contained in this book will provide your child with plenty of opportunities to develop these vital reading comprehension skills. The more your child reads and responds to literature, the greater the improvement you will see in his or her mastery of reading comprehension. To get the most from *Reading Comprehension*, follow these simple steps:

- Provide a comfortable and quiet place for your child to work.
- Encourage your child to work at his or her own pace.
- Help your child with the problems if he or she needs it.
- Offer lots of praise and support.
- Most of all, remember that learning should be fun!

Visit us at *www.flashkidsbooks.com* for free downloads, informative articles, and valuable parent resources!

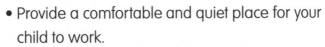

A Brave Bouquet

Imagine hoisting yourself over jagged rocks and scaling steep ledges on a cold mountain. As you climb higher, the air gets thinner and the sun's rays more intense. Just before you reach the snowline at about 10,000 feet, you find what you came looking for. A small, white flower is nestled in craggy rocks. The name of the flower is the "edelweiss," and it only grows in alpine regions.

The alpine region is named after its snow-capped mountains, called the "alps." The French word for "high mountains" is "alpes," which is how mountain ranges like the Swiss Alps and the Himalayan Alps got their names. The habitat of this area is called an "alpine" biome. Plants face many challenges living in this environment. This is why only 200 different kinds of plants can grow there.

Plants rely on oxygen, water, and sunlight to make their own food through the process of photosynthesis. The high altitude in the alps means there is less carbon monoxide, which makes photosynthesis more difficult. The high elevation also brings plants much closer to the sun. The sunlight is more intense and can scorch a plant's leaves. There is little water in alpine areas, so the soil is dry and rocky. You also won't find any high trees because the cold wind would blow them over!

Alpine plants have features that help them survive the harsh alpine conditions. Like all alpine plants, the edelweiss stays close to the ground to avoid the wind. Melted snow is the only source of moisture, and the cold water is deep underground. So the edelweiss grows very deep roots that push down through the rocky soil. The edelweiss leaves have a thick covering that feels like felt. This protects the plant from the wind and the sun's bright rays. All these special features help the plant grow, but it still grows very slowly.

The edelweiss can withstand the alpine conditions, but humans can't. Climbing into the alps is dangerous and difficult. This is why the edelweiss became such a special flower. Long ago, a young man would pick an edelweiss flower to prove his love to a girl. It was risky to climb the rocky cliffs in search of the edelweiss. Many men died while trying, either from falling or from the severe weather. Obtaining the flower proved that the man was physically strong, courageous, and devoted. In fact, the word *edelweiss* means "noble and white" in German. Only a noble person could reach the flower, and its white flowering leaves are like snowflakes—no two are alike.

Alpine plants can't spread seeds, so it's difficult for new plants to grow. Once all the edelweiss flowers are gone in an area, they will not re-grow. Governments help protect the edelweiss by declaring it an endangered plant. You won't find people picking the flowers like they did years ago. Today, the noble thing to do is to admire the white edelweiss and let it continue to grow.

The words in both columns are from the reading passage.

Use context clues to figure out which words have similar meanings.

Draw a line to connect the synonyms.

1. scaling	a. rocky
2. altitude	b. harsh
3. craggy	c. habitat
4. severe	d. climbing
5. biome	e. elevation

Fill in each blank with the correct word from the word box.

snowline	scorch	endangered	photosynthesis
alpine	devoted	noble	withstand

High in the mountains you'll find the 1) _____ biome at about 10,000 feet, just below the 2) _____. There is less carbon monoxide at this altitude, so 3) _____ is more difficult for plants. The sun is more intense and can 4) _____ the plant leaves. The edelweiss is one plant that can 5) _____ the alpine conditions. Young men tried to prove they were 6) _____ by bringing an edelweiss back from the high alps. Only a 7) _____ person could reach the flower. It's difficult for edelweiss to re-grow, so today the plant is 8) _____.

Answer the questions.

1. What are the conditions like in the alpine biome?

   _____

   _____

2. How many types of plants can grow in the alpine biome?

   _____

   _____

3. Why is photosynthesis difficult at high elevations?

   _____

   _____

4. Why do alpine plants stay close to the ground?

   _____

   _____

5. What features help the edelweiss plant survive?

   _____

   _____

6. Why did young men try to pick edelweiss?

   _____

   _____

7. Why is the edelweiss endangered?

   _____

   _____

8. Write the main idea of the passage.

   _____

   _____

   _____

Snuba and Scuba

Colorful fish glide past a swaying sea plant and dart in and out of a beautiful coral reef. Swimmers get a glimpse of this underwater world for just a few moments. Then they must return to the surface and take another breath before plunging underwater again. After all, humans aren't built like fish, and we need air to breathe.

For as long as people have explored the deep sea, they've been searching for a way to linger longer beneath the surface. Long ago, people breathed underwater by using long reeds as if they were straws. Today, we have much more advanced equipment to allow people to stay underwater for long periods of time. Scuba and snuba are two ways that people can "breathe" underwater.

Scuba and snuba divers both breathe air from tanks. Tubes from the tank deliver air to the diver's mouthpiece, called a regulator. The difference between these two methods is where the tank is located. A scuba diver carries the tank on his or her back while swimming. By carrying the air supply, the scuba diver swims freely and can go hundreds of feet deep. With snuba, the swimmer does not wear the air tank. Instead, the tank stays on a raft on the water's surface. A twenty-foot tube brings the air from the raft tank to the swimmer's mouthpiece. The snuba swimmer can breathe underwater, but he or she is always attached to the raft and can only swim twenty feet deep.

A scuba diver has the ultimate underwater freedom, but that freedom comes with a cost. Scuba divers carry equipment that weighs 60 to 75 pounds. Deep water is very cold, so scuba divers must wear wet suits. They also must wear heavy weights to keep from floating back to the water's surface. Learning how to use all this equipment requires a lot of training. A diver begins learning how to use the equipment in a pool, then moves on to open water. When a diver is hundreds of feet deep, it is not possible to swim to the surface quickly or easily. Scuba divers must learn what to do in an emergency. By taking classes, a person can become a certified scuba diver.

Snuba equipment, on the other hand, is very light. The swimmer only needs to wear a mask, the special snuba mouthpiece, a small weight belt, and a harness to connect the airline to the raft. Since there is very little equipment, swimmers can learn snuba quickly. After a few minutes of explanation a swimmer is ready to begin. Snuba swimmers are never more than twenty feet deep, so they can easily swim to the surface in an emergency.

Because of all the gear and training, you must be fifteen years old in order to scuba dive. Snuba, on the other hand, can be done by kids as young as four years old! People of all ages can snuba together without spending a lot of time and money to learn how. That's why snuba is done mainly for fun and recreation. Scuba, however, is done for recreation but also as a profession. Scuba divers repair ships and bridges, do underwater research, take photographs, and even film movies underwater.

Snuba and scuba sound alike, but there are some pretty important differences between the two! Either way, you'll get an amazing and up-close view of the underwater world.

Fill in the chart to show how snuba and scuba are different.

	Snuba	Scuba
1. Where is the air tank?		
2. How deep can the diver go?		
3. Describe the equipment a diver wears.		
4. How much training is needed?		
5. What's the minimum age?		

Write the things that snuba and scuba have in common.

_____

_____

_____

_____

_____

_____

_____

_____

Circle the conclusions that are logical and could be supported with facts from the passage.

List some facts that support the conclusion below.

Conclusion: For a family with young children, snuba is a better activity than scuba.

Support:

_____

_____

_____

_____

_____

_____

Putting the Brakes on Scooters

With the holidays just around the corner, the students at Franklin Elementary School are talking about what presents they hope to get. This year, the item that tops most kids' wish lists is a scooter. The more students talk about scooters, the more teachers become concerned. It's time that Franklin kids hear the facts about scooters!

First of all, there are two different kinds of scooters: foot-powered and motorized. There's nothing wrong with kids riding foot-powered scooters. A foot-powered scooter is much like a traditional bicycle. Instead of sitting and pedaling, the rider stands on a platform and pushes off with one foot to power the scooter. A foot-powered scooter is just as safe as a bike or skateboard as long as the rider is wearing a helmet, knee pads, and elbow pads.

Motorized scooters sometimes look like foot-powered scooters, but there is one huge difference. A motorized scooter has a small gas or electric engine inside of it. Kids don't need to push with their feet to power the scooter—the motor does all the work. It sure sounds like a fun and easy ride, and that's why so many kids are lining up to buy them. But most kids don't even realize that riding these scooters is illegal.

The engine enables a motorized scooter to go much faster than a foot-powered scooter, so it's not safe to ride them on bike paths or sidewalks where other kids are riding non-motorized bikes or scooters. It's also not safe to ride a motorized scooter on roads or highways. A motorized scooter doesn't have brake lights, fenders, or turn signals. Without these safety requirements, scooters can't share the road with cars or motorcycles. Franklin City Police Officer Norton sums it up this way: "On the street, a kid on a scooter is a danger to the other vehicles. On the sidewalks, he's a danger to bikes or normal scooters. And either way, he's a danger to himself."

So where can you ride a motorized scooter? In most cities, you can only ride them on private property. Even in cities where motorized scooters are allowed on some roads, there is a strict age limit. You must be sixteen or older and you must wear a helmet. Basically, if you're not old enough to drive a car, you're not old enough to ride a motorized scooter.

There's one more important thing to remember about motorized scooters. Even though it's illegal for underage kids to ride them, it's not illegal for stores to sell them. Just because you see other kids buying and riding them doesn't make it okay. If you're caught riding a motorized scooter without a license, you could be fined or the scooter could be taken away. Remember, staying off these scooters isn't about ruining your fun, it's about keeping everyone safe.

Use the words in the box to complete the outline.

sidewalk	foot	facts	engine
motorized	lights	himself	sixteen
illegal	private	safety	highways
bicycle	helmet	fined	

I. Introduction

  a) Kids need to hear the 1) _____ about scooters

II. Foot-powered Scooters

  a) Like a 2) _____

  b) Rider pushes with 3) _____

  c) Helmet, knee, and elbow pads must be worn

III. 4) _____ Scooters

  a) Have an 5) _____, so you don't have to push

  b) They are 6) _____ in most cities

IV. Why Motorized Scooters Are Unsafe

  a) They go too fast to be ridden on the 7) _____

  b) Not safe to ride on 8) _____ with cars

  c) No brake 9) _____ , turn signals, or fenders

  d) Rider is a danger to 10) _____ and to others

V. Restrictions

  a) Only allowed on 11) _____ property

  b) Must be 12) _____ or older

  c) Must wear a 13) _____

VI. Conclusion

  a) Stores still sell scooters

  b) If caught you'll be 14) _____

  c) 15) _____ is the key

Circle the correct answer.

1. The audience for this article is _____.
   a) students
   b) teachers
   c) police officers

2. The purpose of this article is to _____.
   a) explain why kids like riding scooters so much
   b) convince kids to buy foot-powered scooters
   c) warn kids that motorized scooters are illegal and unsafe

3. The tone of this article is _____.
   a) humorous
   b) serious
   c) sad

4. The article includes a quote from a police officer to _____.
   a) reinforce that motorized scooters are dangerous
   b) support kids who want to ride motorized scooters
   c) make fun of kids who ride motorized scooters

5. Summarize the author's main point.

_____

_____

_____

_____

_____

_____

_____

_____

_____

_____

All Shook Up

An alarm blasted through the house. Everyone jolted out of bed and took cover under the nearest table or desk. When the alarm stopped, they hurried outside to the family's meeting place.

"That took almost five minutes!" Laura said, clutching her stopwatch. "During a real earthquake, that would be way too long!"

"It's just a drill," her mother said. "The important thing is that everyone knows the plan."

Ever since her class started studying earthquakes, Laura had been making her family do a lot of earthquake drills. She worried about being in a real earthquake. The more she worried, the more drills she did.

They had spent weeks earthquake-proofing the house. Laura and her mother bolted all the shelves and mirrors to the wall and had put latches on all the cabinet doors to keep dishes from falling out. They had also moved all the beds so they weren't beneath any windows or heavy pictures. Everyone in the family knew how to shut off the water and gas, and they had even practiced using the fire extinguisher.

"I know," Laura said, "but it's still scary to think about a real quake happening."

"Earthquakes are no big deal," Byron said with a big yawn. "It's just some energy being released from deep in the earth." Byron smirked as everyone went back inside.

That night, the family heard a loud rumbling. The kitchen table started to vibrate, and the hanging plant swayed.

Byron screamed as he dove under a chair. Everyone ducked under the nearest table, just as they had practiced. Laura was surprised at how calm she felt. She had barely felt the shaking and it lasted only a few seconds.

"I thought the shaking would never stop!" Byron said. His face was pale and his hands trembled.

"The shaking," their dad said, "wasn't even a real earthquake. It was that large moving van driving by."

Sure enough, a big van was pulling up next door. Laura and her parents laughed at their mistake.

Draw arrows to show how each event led to the next.

One night the family heard a loud rumbling.

Laura realized that she was prepared and didn't need to be afraid.

Laura learned about earthquakes in school.

She earthquake-proofed the house and made her family do drills.

Laura worried about earthquakes a lot.

Answer the questions.

1. How did Laura's attitude about earthquakes change?

_____

_____

2. What did Laura's parents do to help her get over her fear of earthquakes?

_____

_____

3. How did Byron and Laura react differently when they thought there was an earthquake? _____

_____

4. What would you do in a real earthquake?

_____

_____

5. Circle the sentence that best expresses the story's theme:
   a) Being prepared helps you stay calm in an emergency.
   b) There is no way to prepare for a real emergency.
   c) Being afraid of earthquakes is silly.

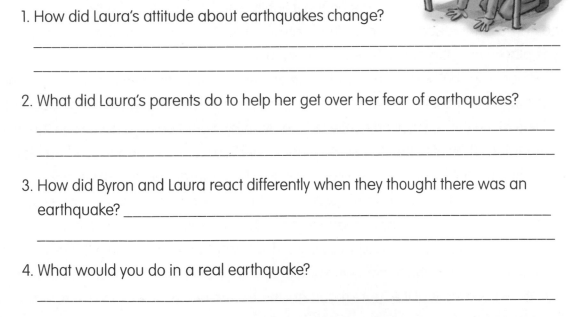

Egyptian Mummies

The ancient Egyptians believed that after a person died, their soul would be reunited with their body in the afterlife. They thought that the journey to the afterlife was long and dangerous, so Egyptians had special burial and funeral practices to make sure that the person would be able to complete the trip.

The first step was to embalm, or preserve, the dead body by making a mummy. It took 70 days to mummify a body. The embalmers started by removing all the organs, including the stomach, intestine, liver, lungs, and even the brain. In fact, the embalmers used a special hook that allowed them to pull the brain out of the person's nose! A special salt was used to dry out the organs. Then each organ was put in a different jar.

After all of the organs were removed, the embalmers washed the body and let it dry for 40 days. Then it was time to wrap the body in cloth. They covered the whole body in linen shrouds, or garments, and bound it tightly with linen strips. Oftentimes, they wrote the name of the dead person on the shrouds. Once the body was mummified, a mask was placed over the person's head and shoulders.

Preserving the body was only the beginning of the burial ceremony. The mummy was placed in a coffin that would help protect it in the afterlife. By painting eyes on the outside of the coffin, Egyptians believed the mummy would be able to see into the world of the living. They also painted spells, chants, and good luck charms called amulets on the coffin. Then they placed each coffin inside a larger tomb for more protection.

Taking the coffin to the tomb was part of the funeral procession. A procession is when people march or walk in a long line. The embalmer took the coffin on a boat across the Nile River. Priests followed behind, carrying the jars that held the organs. The friends and family of the person who had died were waiting on the other side of the river. Egyptians believed that the more mourners there were at the funeral, the more important the person was. Families sometimes hired mourners to cry at the funeral!

If the person who had died was very wealthy, their tomb would be a large pyramid. Tombs were also carved out of cliffs or built underground. The tomb not only held the coffin, but it was also filled with the person's favorite possessions. King Tut's tomb, for example, had hunting weapons, games, chairs, makeup, food, statues, sandals, clothes, and even couches inside!

Small statues called shabti were also placed inside the tomb. Egyptians believed that in the afterlife, the shabti statues would come to life and act as servants. It was common for people to be buried with several hundred shabti statues. This way, there would be one servant for each day of the year and thirty-six servants to supervise!

The embalming process preserved the mummies for thousands of years. Historians can still read the writing on the outside of mummies' coffins and figure out who is inside. As historians study the burial ceremony, they learn about life in ancient Egypt. The coffin decorations and the items found inside tombs teach us about Egyptian beliefs. Thanks to mummies, we know what ancient Egypt was like!

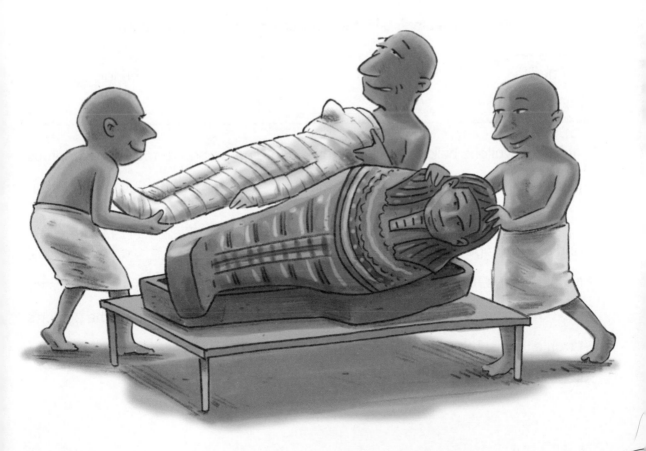

The words in both columns are from the reading passage.

Use context clues to figure out which words have similar meanings.

Draw a line to connect the synonyms.

1. embalm

2. cloth

3. amulet

4. procession

5. journey

a. preserve

b. trip

c. linen

d. long line

e. good luck charm

Fill in each blank with the correct word from the word box.

afterlife	embalmer	coffin	burial
mummify	organs	tomb	shrouds

Ancient Egyptians believed that after a person died he had to make a dangerous journey to the 1) _____. So the 2) _____ had an important job of preserving the body. He removed all the 3) _____ , let the body dry, and then wrapped it in 4) _____. To 5) _____ a body like this, it took 70 days. The 6) _____ was decorated with pictures and spells for protection. Then it was placed inside a 7) _____ , along with the person's favorite things. This special 8) _____ ceremony has helped historians learn important things about Egyptian culture.

Answer the questions.

1. What did Egyptians believe about the afterlife?_____
_____

2. Why were eyes painted on the outside of the coffin?_____
_____

3. Why would an Egyptian hire professional mourners for the funeral?
_____
_____

4. What different types of tombs were used?_____
_____

5. Why did Egyptians place shabti statues inside the tombs?
_____
_____

6. What were some of the things found inside King Tut's tomb?
_____
_____

7. How do the mummies help historians learn about Egypt?
_____
_____

8. Number the events to show the correct sequence.
___ Embalmers and priests took the coffin across the Nile
___ They decorated the coffin.
___ The body was wrapped in cloth.
___ Embalmers removed the organs and put them in jars
___ The body was washed and then let dry for 40 days.
___ They placed the coffin inside a tomb along with the
    person's favorite things.

A Fair Deal

Visit the Pinewood County Fair and Help Pinewood Schools!

Zoom down a rollercoaster, sing along with live music, and munch on the best snacks in the whole county. The Pinewood Pass is the best way to see the attractions at this year's county fair. You can buy a Pinewood Pass at any elementary school in the county. You'll feel great knowing that 10% of the price is donated back to the school! That's why the Pinewood Pass is approved by the Pinewood Parents Association. Here's what you get with the Pinewood Pass:

- 2 days admission to the fair
- 50 Ride coupons (most rides require about 5 coupons)
- Admission to the petting zoo
- Tickets to see a live music show
- All-you-can-eat hot dogs
- Free refills on soda

The cost of the Pinewood Pass is $10.00 per adult and $5.00 per child. The Pinewood Pass will not be sold at the fair. You must purchase the pass in advance at any elementary school in the county. Here's what the people of Pinewood have to say about the Pinewood Pass:

"I bought the Pinewood Pass last year and it worked great for the whole family! Being able to spend 2 days at the fair is worth the price!"
—Olivia Burke, Pinewood parent

"I always buy the Pinewood Pass because I know that some of the money goes to help Pinewood Schools."
—Chuck Kelly, Pinewood parent and teacher

"The Pinewood Pass has everything I need! There are enough ride coupons to go on every ride, and I can have as many hot dogs as I want!"
—Carson Moore, seventh-grader

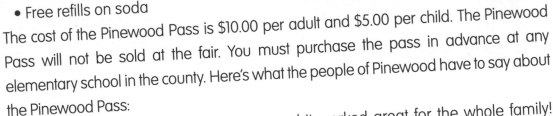

The Pinewood County Fair Is Coming!

There's no limit to the fun you'll have with the Fair Fun Wristband. You won't have to bother with ride coupons. Just slip on a wristband and you'll have unlimited access to almost everything at the fair! What could be better than a whole day of thrilling rides, tasty food, and amazing performances? With the Fair Fun Wristband, you won't miss out on a thing. Here's what you'll get with your wristband:

- One-day admission to the fair
- Unlimited rides
- Unlimited hot dogs and drink refills
- Tickets to the evening magic show
- Admission to the petting zoo
- Front row seats at the pig races

You must buy your wristband in advance. The price is $20.00 per person. The price for adults and children is the same. You cannot buy wristbands at the fair.

You can buy your wristband at any of the following Pinewood locations:

- Pinewood Pet Store
- Hamilton's Grocery Store
- Fast Fuel Gas Stations
- Kidsworld Toy Store
- Superbooks

Fill in the Venn Diagram to show the similarities and differences between the Pinewood Pass and the Fair Fun Wristband.

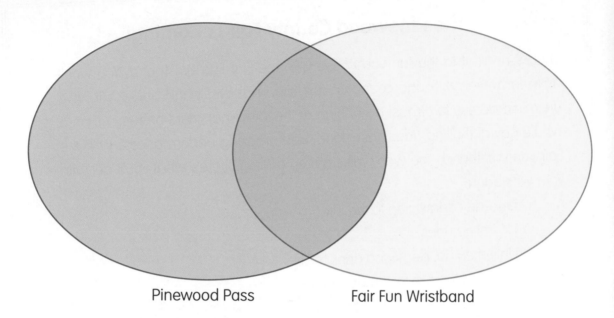

Pinewood Pass   Fair Fun Wristband

**Circle the conclusions that are logical and could be supported
with facts from the flyers.**

The Fair Fun Wristband is more expensive than Pinewood Pass.

The county fair does not have enough food booths or rides this year.

If you like using ride coupons, you should buy a wristband.

You cannot buy the wristband or the pass at the fair.

If you like live music more than magic,
you should buy the Pinewood Pass.

List some facts that support the conclusion below.

Conclusion: Many parents in Pinewood support the Pinewood Pass.

Support:

_____

_____

_____

_____

_____

A Very Hot Hot Dog

Have you ever walked outside barefoot on a hot summer day? You probably hopped across the scorching pavement and your feet felt like they were burning! How did the pavement get so hot? The sun heated it! The sun gives off so much heat, in fact, that it can also be a source of power. Energy produced by the sun is called solar power, and people are finding all sorts of ways to use it.

Solar energy can be used to heat a whole house! You might have seen large shiny panels on the roofs of some houses. Those panels convert the sunlight into electricity, which provides heat to the house. Have you noticed that most calculators don't use normal batteries? That's because they are solar powered. As soon as light hits the calculator, it turns on. Solar energy can even be used to cook food! Read on to find out how to make your own solar hot dog cooker.

The only items you need to build your solar cooker are a cardboard box, tin foil, poster board, tape, glue, and a coat hanger. The cardboard box is going to collect the sun's heat. To do this, you first need to create a parabola. A parabola is a curve or dip. If you've watched rain falling outside, you might have seen the water collect into gutters. Gutters are curved dips in the ground. A parabola is just like that. It helps collect and concentrate the sun's energy.

To make a parabolic curve in your box, place the box with the open end facing up. Trace a curved line along the two long sides of the box. Make sure that the lowest point in the dip is in the middle of the box. Ask a parent to use a knife to cut out the curve on each side of the box. Now you're going to cover the top of the box. Measure and cut a piece of poster board that will fit exactly over the open part of the box. Use tape to attach the poster board to the box.

Glue a layer of tin foil to the poster board. Make sure the shiny side is facing up. Avoid wrinkling the foil and keep it as smooth as possible. The foil will reflect the sun's light and help trap the heat inside the cooker. When you place your cooker in the sun, a bright spot should shine where the light is concentrated. This is the focal point.

Now it's time to set up a roasting stick. The stick should hover over the focal point, so you'll need some side support. Tape some scrap cardboard to the sides of the box at the lowest point in the curve. The top of the side support should be a few inches above the curved box edge. After putting a hot dog on a hanger or skewer, push it through the cardboard supports. Your hot dog will be right above the focal point, soaking up the sun's heat. Watch your hot dog cook, then remove it and enjoy!

It's a lot of fun to roast your own hot dog using the sun. But the best thing about solar energy isn't that you can make your own solar cooker. It's the fact that, unlike energy sources like coal or oil, the sun's energy is renewable. That means it's unlimited and will never run out! So as you munch on your tasty hot dog, you can feel good about tapping into this incredible energy source.

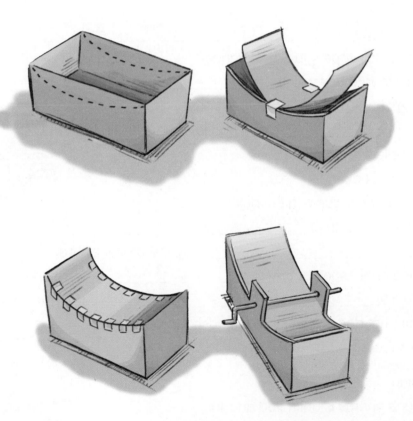

Use the words in the box to complete the outline.

focal point	tin foil	cardboard box	poster board	parabola
collect	panels	solar	roasting	renewable

I. Introduction

    a) Energy produced by the sun is called 1) _____ power

II. Examples of Solar Power

    a) Roof 2) _____ convert sunlight into
       energy for a house

    b) A solar calculator

    c) Solar cookers

III. Solar Cooking

    a) Items needed: 3) _____, poster
       board, tin foil, tape, glue, coat hanger

    b) The cardboard box will 4) _____
       the sun's heat

    c) A 5) _____ is a curve or dip that
       helps collect the sunlight

IV. Building the Cooker

    a) Cut a parabolic curve in the box

    b) Cover the top with 6) _____

    c) Glue 7) _____ to the poster board

    d) Find the bright spot, or 8) _____, of the cooker

    e) Set up a 9) _____ stick with cardboard supports

    f) Put your hot dog on the stick and push it through
       the cardboard

V. Conclusion

    a) The sun's energy is unlimited and 10)

    _____

Answer the questions.

1. The audience for this passage is _____ .
   a) hot dog companies
   b) scientists who study the sun
   c) kids and others interested in solar energy

2. The purpose of this passage is to _____ .
   a) warn people that using solar power is dangerous and should not be tried at home
   b) inform people about solar power and teach them how to make a solar cooker
   c) convince kids that hot dogs are important and everyone should learn to cook them

3. The tone of this passage is _____ .
   a) somber
   b) humorous
   c) informative

4. The speaker most likely thinks that _____ .
   a) coal and oil are better sources of energy than solar power
   b) it's important to use renewable sources of energy, such as solar power
   c) the sun is very powerful, but we have not figured out how to use its power

5. Explain how to build a solar cooker.

_____

_____

_____

_____

_____

_____

_____

A Special Birthday

Kristine awoke to the sound of soft chanting. As she went to the window, she noticed her friend Keikko was already awake.

"Today is a very special day," said Keikko, "It's April 8th, and here in Japan we celebrate Buddha's birthday."

Keikko grinned as she handed Kristine a Japanese kimono and helped her get dressed. The girls went downstairs where the rest of the family was dressed in kimonos too. They were making beautiful flower arrangments.

"'Hana Matsuri' means 'flower festival,'" Keikko explained to Kristine. "According to Buddhist belief, Buddha was born in a garden. Colorful flowers remind us of his birth."

The girls heard lots of noise in the street. They ran outside to join a lively parade. Most people carried flowers, but some had decorated floats. One of the floats had a huge white elephant with a small house on its back. Inside the house was a small statue.

"That's a statue of Buddha," Keikko explained. "He spent most his life in India, so that's why the statue is on an elephant."

The parade wound its way through the streets and ended at the Buddhist temple. Kristine noticed some people pouring something over a Buddha statue's head. Keikko explained that Buddhists believe that sweet tea rained from heaven and baptized Buddha on the day he was born. People pour sweet tea on the statue's head as a symbol of this.

After they finished at the temple, Kristine followed Keikko and her family as they carried beautiful lanterns to the river. Keikko passed Kristine a piece of paper for writing a special wish or desire. Keikko wrote a wish for peace and happiness on her lantern.

Kristine knew exactly what she wanted to write on her lantern. She wished to always remember this special day at the Hana Matsuri festival in Japan. Kristine put her lantern in the river with the others, and watched it slowly float into the night.

Draw a line to connect each event from Buddha's life
with the tradition it relates to on his birthday.

1. Buddha lived most of his life in India.
2. Buddha was born in a garden.
3. Buddhists believe that sweet tea rained from heaven the day he was born.

a) People pour sweet tea on a statue of Buddha's head.
b) Buddha's birthday is called the "festival of flowers."
c) A statue of Buddha rides on an elephant in the parade.

Answer the questions.

1. What is the relationship between Kristine and Keikko?

_____

_____

2. What does "Hana Matsuri" mean?

_____

_____

3. What do the girls do to celebrate Buddha's birthday?

_____

_____

4. What does Kristine wish for on her lantern note?

_____

_____

_____

5. Circle the sentence that best describes the story's setting:
   a) The setting of the story is an ancient Japanese village.
   b) The story takes place at the time Buddha was born.
   c) The story takes place in Japan on Buddha's birthday.

Hammurabi's Code

Imagine if you lived in a city where none of the laws were written down. You might be arrested for something that you didn't even know was illegal! With nothing recorded, the leaders could change the laws and punishments as they pleased. This is what life was like in many ancient city-states. There were no written laws to protect people.

Around 1750 BC, King Hammurabi of Babylonia wrote one of the earliest sets of laws. Before King Hammurabi, a few other kings had written down short lists of laws for their own cities. But King Hammurabi wrote a very long, detailed set of laws that applied to his entire empire. His collection of 282 laws is known as Hammurabi's Code.

The writing system during this time was called cuneiform, and the symbols were very complicated. The English alphabet and punctuation system includes about 64 symbols. Cuneiform had over 600 symbols! Plus, it couldn't be written with ink and paper. Each symbol had to be chiseled into stone.

The laws were carved into stone columns that were eight feet high. The columns were then displayed for everyone in the city to see. Nobody could claim they didn't know about the rules or punishments. They were final. The leaders also could not change the laws. This is where the phrase "written in stone" comes from, meaning that something is final and unchangeable.

Hammurabi's Code begins with an introduction that lists all the city-states the King had conquered. This way, it was clear that everyone in the empire was to obey these laws. The introduction also explains that the purpose of the laws is to bring about justice for all the people. King Hammurabi explains that laws help make for a good government. Following the introduction is a list of 282 laws.

King Hammurabi covered a wide range of topics in his Code. Many of the laws deal with stealing, and the punishment was usually cruel. Breaking into someone's house was punished by death, as was any type of robbery. One law even explains that if someone steals from a house while the house is on fire, the thief should be thrown into the fire. The harsh punishments for stealing show how important owning property was during this time.

Many of the laws are based on a concept people call "an eye for an eye." This means the punishment should be equal to the crime. For example, one of the laws in the Code says that if a man breaks another man's bones, his bones should be broken. Another law says that if a house collapses and kills the owner's son, then the man who built the house should have his own son killed in return. The laws also made people accountable for their work. The builder was responsible for the quality of the house. If a sailor damaged a ship because he wasn't paying attention, the Code says he had to compensate, or pay, the ship's owner.

Hammurabi's Code includes laws about trade and business, marriage and divorce, and even farming and gardening. One law states that if a man's wife becomes sick, he must take care of her until she dies. The laws also gave instructions to doctors, farmers, slaves, merchants, inn keepers, and even barbers on how to do their jobs correctly.

King Hammurabi ruled for 42 years and had a vast empire. By writing down the laws he not only protected his people, he also paved the way for other civilizations to develop written laws.

The words in both columns are from the reading passage.

Use context clues to figure out which words have similar meanings.

Draw a line to connect the synonyms.

1. chiseled

2. accountable

3. written in stone

4. cruel

5. compensate

a. harsh

b. pay

c. responsible

d. final

e. carved

Fill in each blank with the correct word.

| Babylonia | columns | instructions | justice |
| Code | crimes | quality | punishment |

King Hammurabi of 1) _____ wrote the first detailed set of laws around 1750 BC. His collection of laws is called Hammurabi's 2) _____. He had a very large empire, and he wanted everyone to live by the same rules. The laws were carved into large stone 3) _____ and displayed where everyone could see. The laws explained how to punish people who committed different 4) _____. 5) It was important that the _____ be equal to the crime. The Code also gave 6) _____ telling people how to do their jobs. If the 7) _____ of someone's work was not good, he had to make it right. These written laws helped protect people and give them 8) _____ .

Answer the questions.

1. How was Hammurabi's Code new and different?

_____

_____

2. What is cuneiform and how is it different from English?

_____

_____

3. What did King Hammurabi write about in the introduction to his Code?

_____

_____

4. Why does Hammurabi's Code have such harsh punishments for stealing?

_____

_____

5. What does the phrase "an eye for an eye" mean, and what are some examples of it in Hammurabi's Code?

_____

_____

6. Where does the phrase "written in stone" come from?

_____

_____

7. How do laws protect people?

_____

_____

8. Write the main idea of the passage.

_____

_____

Athens and Sparta

In ancient Greece, the city-states of Athens and Sparta shared the same language, religion, and customs. And yet, Spartans and Athenians led very different lives. These two cities had different ideas about education, family life, and politics.

Growing up in Sparta meant learning to become a soldier. At the age of seven, boys were sent to away to military schools. These schools focused on developing the boys' physical strength and making them tough soldiers. While the Spartan boys were learning obedience and discipline, boys in Athens learned reading, writing, math, and even music. In Athens it was important for boys to learn about poetry and drama and to appreciate the arts. This is why about half of the men in Athens could read, but most Spartans were illiterate.

In Sparta, the military controlled every aspect of life. At the age of 20, boys finished training and became soldiers in the army. Even if a Spartan soldier got married, he could not live with his wife until he turned 30. He continued to serve in the military until he was 60 years old. Boys in Athens served in the army for two years only, from the ages of 18 to 20. After that, they could choose to be a solider, or they could be an artist, a teacher, a craftsman, or a merchant. Family life was important to Athenians, so families lived together and were not separated.

In both Sparta and Athens, girls did not have the same opportunities as boys. But the Spartans did believe that women needed to be strong in order to give birth to strong soldiers. So, Spartan girls were trained to be physically strong and tough. Spartan women had a great deal of freedom because their husbands lived away from home with the army. In Athens, as in most of the cities of ancient Greece, women were expected to stay indoors. Girls were not given much education and did not have much freedom.

The governments in Sparta and Athens did have some similar features. Both cities had an Assembly, which was a group of leaders who helped run the city. Also, both Spartans and Athenians elected the members of the Assembly. The Spartan Assembly, however, actually did not have very much power. There were two kings in Sparta. There were also the ephors—a group of five men who held most of the power and ran the military and government as they chose. The people of Athens wanted the exact opposite.

They believed that no one group of people should hold all the power, so they elected members of the Assembly every year. People voted on new laws, and they debated and discussed lots of issues.

When it came to how Sparta and Athens interacted with their neighboring cities, their politics were surprisingly different. Sparta did have a strong army, but they weren't very interested in attacking their neighbors. They liked to keep to themselves and be independent. They had a simple life, and did not desire fine things and luxuries. Athens, on the other hand, was always looking outward. They traded with other cities and enjoyed collecting fine things. As they saw other lands, they hungered to conquer their neighbors.

Athenians and Spartans were both proud of their identity, and they believed that their way of life was the best. It's no wonder that they eventually went to war with one another. Sparta won the war, but the Spartan soldiers did not burn Athens. They let the culture of Athens live on, with the understanding that Athens would not attack other cities.

Fill in the chart to show how Sparta and Athens were different.

	Sparta	Athens
1. How were boys educated?		
2. What type of military service was expected?		
3. How were girls treated?		
4. What type of government did they have?		
5. How did they interact with neighboring cities?		

Write some things that Sparta and Athens have in common.

_____

_____

_____

Circle the conclusions that are logical and could be supported with facts from the passage.

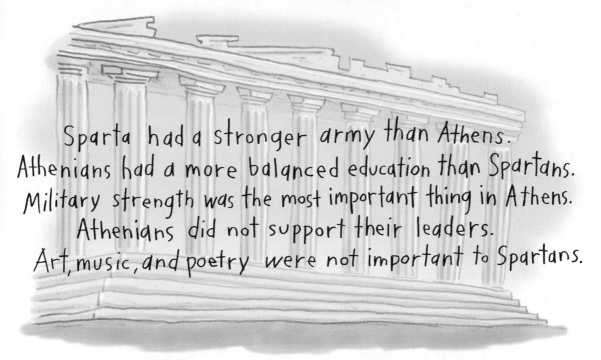

Sparta had a stronger army than Athens.
Athenians had a more balanced education than Spartans.
Military strength was the most important thing in Athens.
Athenians did not support their leaders.
Art, music, and poetry were not important to Spartans.

List some facts that support the conclusion below.

Conclusion: Athenians were more creative than Spartans.

Support:

_____

_____

_____

_____

_____

_____

Lighting up the Sky

Dear Mom and Dad,

I'm having a great time at Camp Falling Star! Last night I learned how the camp got its name. All the campers slept outside and watched the sky. We didn't get much sleep, though, because bright flashes of light appeared in the sky all night long. People used to think these lights were falling stars, and they named the camp after it. But they weren't falling stars—they were meteors!

I learned that stars and meteors are actually very different. Stars are bigger than planets, and they don't break into pieces or fall out of the sky. A meteor is a streak of light that occurs when tiny, pebble-sized meteoroids heat up and vaporize, leaving a glowing trail. The camp counselors taught us all about where meteors come from and how they light up the night sky.

It all starts with comets. I always pictured a comet as a flaming fireball, but a comet is actually a ball of ice and rock. As it zooms through the sky and nears the sun, specks of rock and dust melt off. Comets are big and travel so fast that they shed about 55 tons of dust specks every second! This creates a long tail that follows behind the comet. Years after the comet has passed, the trail of dust particles still lingers in space.

As the Earth orbits around the sun, sometimes it travels through these leftover clouds of comet dust. Each speck of the dust is a meteoroid traveling faster than 100,000 miles per hour. The Earth's gravity pulls the meteoroids close to the Earth. When a meteoroid hits the Earth's atmosphere, it burns up. So each flash of light I saw in the sky was a tiny dust particle exploding!

The meteors I saw last night were part of what's called the Perseid meteor shower. It was caused by Comet Swift-Tuttle, which sweeps through our solar system every 130 years. The last time it passed the Earth, in 1992, it left behind plenty of dust specks. Every August, the Earth runs into this cloud of comet dust. Most of the meteors appear around the star constellation of Perseus. That's why the shower is named the Perseid Meteor Shower.

Meteor showers are special because you can see lots of meteors in one night. Sometimes I saw 50 or even 100 in a single hour! There were also slow times, when I only saw a few each hour. I didn't need a telescope or binoculars to see the meteors. I just laid on my back and looked up to see bright streaks of light race across the sky. The bright glow of each meteor only lasted a couple of seconds. Each one was spectacular to see!

The Perseid Meteor Shower can be seen most of the month of August. I wish that you both could see it! There are too many lights in the city to see the meteors. You have to drive up into the mountains where it's very dark. The best time to spot them is between midnight and dawn. I want to come back to Camp Falling Star every summer and see the meteor shower!

Sincerely,
Nick

Use the words in the box to complete the outline.

telescope	tail	shower	Perseus
rice	ice	atmosphere	meteors
dust	gravity	August	midnight

I. Introduction

   a) Camp Falling Star is actually named after 1) _____

II. Stars and Meteors

   a) Stars are big and don't fall from the sky

   b) Meteors are as small as grains of

     2) _____

III. Comets

   a) Made of 3) _____

   and rock

   b) The sun melts off particles, which form a 4) _____

   c) The tail lingers even after the comet passes

IV. Meteor

   a) A meteor is a piece of comet 5) _____

   b) As the Earth orbits the sun, it runs into dust clouds

   c) Earth's 6) _____ pulls the meteors in

   d) The dust particles explode when they hit the Earth's 7) _____

   e) As the meteor burns, you see a flash of light

V. Perseid Meteor 8) _____

   a) Caused by Comet Tuttle-Swift, passes Earth every 130 years

   b) During 9) _____, the Earth runs into the comet's tail

   c) Named after the constellation 10) _____

VI. Watching a Meteor Shower

   a) Number of meteors per hour ranges from a few to 100 per hour

   b) No 11) _____ or binoculars needed

   c) Must be in a dark place

   d) Between 12) _____ and dawn is the best time

Answer the questions.

1. The audience for this letter is _____ .
   a) kids at Camp Falling Star
   b) Nick's parents
   c) meteorologists

2. The purpose of this passage is to _____ .
   a) teach people how to use telescopes for the Perseid Meteor Shower
   b) convince people to pay more attention to meteor showers
   c) share the experience of watching a meteor shower and explain how
      they happen

3. The tone of this passage is _____ .
   a) upbeat and informative
   b) sarcastic and funny
   c) angry and forceful

4. Based on this letter, we know that Nick probably enjoys _____ .
   a) taking showers
   b) camping and studying the stars
   c) traveling to the city

5. Summarize how meteor showers happen:

_____

_____

_____

_____

_____

_____

_____

_____

A Day at the Races

Bruno pushed his way though a crowd of people to get a look at the racetrack. It was his first time at the Circus Maximus, and he gazed at the huge oval track below. Pretty soon, horse-drawn chariots would be speeding around the track!

Bruno looked around frantically for his brother Anthony, who had wandered off into the maze of shops and arcades. He finally found Anthony at a souvenir stand, buying a statue of a charioteer named Diocles.

The two boys pressed through crowds until they reached the spectator stands. Bruno noticed that the stands were almost full, so spectators were now gathering on the hills behind the Circus Maximus to get a glimpse of the race. Some fans were dressed all in red, white, blue, or green to show support for their favorite team. Bruno and Anthony wore red wristbands because their favorite charioteer, Diocles, drove for the Reds.

A murmur went through the crowd as the emperor stepped out of his palace. Bruno and Anthony knew that the race must be about to begin. Music filled the air as a parade started on the track below. The charioteers and teams led the way, with musicians and dancers trailing behind. The crowd cheered for the games to begin, and the charioteers drew lots to determine their starting positions.

As the drivers boarded their chariots and waited behind the starting gates, the crowd buzzed with talk of who would win. Then a white cloth was dropped on the field, and the gates burst open. The chariot race had begun! The horses flew onto the track, pulling their chariots behind. Bruno watched the charioteers bounce up and down as they raced around the track. Diocles had the horse reins wrapped around his waist to keep from flying out of the chariot. The crowd roared as the chariots rounded the corners.

On the seventh lap, Diocles got the lead. Everyone cheered as the trumpeter played to signal the end of the race. Diocles had won! The emperor gave Diocles a palm branch and a wreath of laurel leaves. Bruno and Anthony waved red scarves to celebrate the red team's victory. Bruno knew he would be returning to watch the chariot races again and again.

Draw a line to connect each cause with its effect.

1. The stands were filling up.

2. A white cloth was dropped on the field.

3. Diocles won the race.

a) The gates opened and the race began.

b) The emperor gave him a palm branch and wreath.

c) Spectators were gathering on the hills behind the stands.

Answer the questions.

1. Where did Bruno find his brother Anthony?

_____

_____

_____

_____

2. What were the four teams that charioteers could drive for?

_____

_____

3. How did the charioteers keep from flying out of the chariot?

_____

_____

4. What happened at the end of the race?

_____

_____

5. Circle the sentence that best describes the story's setting:

   a) The story's setting is modern-day Greece.

   b) The story takes place at the Circus Maximus in ancient Rome.

   c) The setting of the story is the Roman Coliseum.

The Story of Sneakers

What kind of shoes are you wearing today? If you're like many American kids, you laced up a pair of sneakers before running out the door this morning. It's no surprise that each American buys an average of two pairs of sneakers a year. With the wide variety of sneaker styles, almost everyone can find a pair that they like. Plus, sneakers are comfortable, lightweight, and offer lots of support for your feet. Where did these shoes come from, and how did they get such a funny name?

The sneaker was actually invented by accident. A man named Charles Goodyear owned a rubber company, and he was trying to create a waterproof mailbag for the postal service. People's mail got wet whenever it rained, so Goodyear was trying to make a canvas bag that was covered in rubber. But he couldn't get the rubber to stick to the canvas because the texture was either too soft or too hard. Frustrated by his failed attempts, one day Goodyear shook a spoonful of gummy rubber, and a glob of it landed on the hot stove. When he peeled the rubber off the stove, he realized the heat had changed it. The rubber was now strong and flexible. Goodyear's discovery not only helped him make his canvas and rubber mailbag, it also led to the invention of canvas shoes with rubber soles that we call sneakers.

The rubber sole was the key to what made sneakers special and how they got their name. People liked how the shoe gripped the ground and called them "gumshoes" because of the elastic rubber sole. They were also called "croquet shoes" because they were perfect for leisure activities like tennis and croquet.

When a new brand called Keds hit the market in 1917, the name "sneakers" was born. Other shoes at this time were still heavy and clunky, so they made a lot of noise as people walked. But the rubber soles on Keds made it possible for people to walk very quietly. Wearing these noiseless shoes, a person could sneak by without being heard. Some people even called them "creepers" because they allowed thieves to creep quietly through the house!

Another name for sneakers was "chucks," after a basketball player named Chuck Taylor. His name was printed on high top sneakers called Converse All Stars, so kids started calling their sneakers "chucks." Converse All Stars became very popular, and they are still sold today. In fact, 60% of Americans have owned at least one pair of Converse All Stars, making them the most popular sneaker in history!

For many years, people wore sneakers only when playing sports or for recreation. Sneakers were too casual for work, school, or even to go out shopping. Then in the 1950s, sneakers became part of the youth culture. A famous actor named James Dean was photographed wearing sneakers, jeans, and a white tee shirt. Teenagers everywhere wanted to copy the look. Wearing sneakers was a way for young people to express themselves. Pretty soon, sneakers weren't just for the playing field or the tennis court. People wore them just about anywhere: to school, the office, and even parties. One rock and roll singer made history when he got married wearing a pair of sneakers!

Whether we call them croquet shoes, sneakers, creepers, or chucks, we can all agree that Americans love their sneakers. In fact, we spend 13 billion dollars a year on sneakers!

The words in both columns are from the reading passage.

Use context clues to figure out which words have similar meanings.

Draw a line to connect the synonyms.

1. flexible	a. creep
2. leisure	b. quiet
3. sole	c. shoe bottom
4. sneak	d. recreation
5. noiseless	e. elastic

Fill in each blank with the correct word.

lightweight	Goodyear	creepers	casual
rubber	flexible	teenagers	recreation

Americans love wearing sneakers because they are comfortable and
1) _____. What makes sneakers special is the 2) _____
sole. A man named Charles 3) _____ accidentally flung a glob of
rubber on the hot stove. The heat made the rubber 4) _____enough
to attach to canvas. People called the shoes 5) _____ because the
rubber soles made them quiet. Back then, sneakers were only worn for sports or
6) _____. In the 1950s, 7) _____ started wearing sneakers
all the time. Even though sneakers are 8) _____, people today wear
them just about anywhere!

Answer the questions.

1. Why was Goodyear having a hard time making a waterproof mailbag?

   _____

   _____

2. What did Goodyear discover about rubber?

   _____

   _____

3. At first, what did people call these shoes with rubber soles?

   _____

   _____

4. How was the name "sneakers" born?

   _____

   _____

5. Why did people call their sneakers "chucks"?

   _____

   _____

6. What is the most popular sneaker of all time?

   _____

   _____

7. How did teenagers feel about sneakers in the 1950s?

   _____

   _____

8. Write the main idea of the passage.

   _____

   _____

   _____

   _____

   _____

Animal Roommates

Have you ever had to share your room? Perhaps your roommate snored all night long and always left stuff on the floor. As a result, you couldn't get any sleep and the room was always messy. The arrangement probably didn't work out very well. On the other hand, perhaps your roommate was good at math, and you were a great reader. As you helped each other out, you both benefited from living together.

In nature, two different animals often end up being roommates as well. We call this symbiosis, which is a Greek word that means "to live together." Just like human roommates, sometimes one animal causes problems for the other. The troublemaker is a parasite, and this living arrangement is called parasitism. The parasite gets all the perks, and the other animal gets the bad end of the deal. Other times, the arrangement works out well for both animals. This is called mutualism because both animals benefit from living together.

A tick is a good example of a parasite. Ticks can be found in fields of tall grass. Ticks perch atop the tall blades and wait for an animal like a rhino to walk by. Rhinos often stop to munch on the grass, making it easy for ticks to climb aboard. Once a tick is attached to the rhino, it bites into the rhino's skin. The tick burrows deep in the rhino's skin and sucks its blood. This relationship can be described as parasitism. The tick gets a tasty meal from sucking the rhino's blood, but the rhino gets nothing in return. In fact, ticks carry diseases that can spread to the rhinos when they bite them. The rhino is actually harmed by having the tick as a roommate.

Picture a rhino snarling and growling as he feels ticks biting into his skin. The rhino can't reach behind its ears or on the back of its neck. He has no way to get the ticks off his back! Fortunately, the rhino has another roommate who can help him out. The tickbird also likes to climb aboard the rhino, but the tickbird is not a parasite. In fact, in Swahili the name for a tickbird is *askari wa kifaru,* which means "the rhino's guard." The tickbird helps out the rhino by picking the ticks off its back. The rhino gets these nasty pests removed, and the tickbird gets a tasty meal! It's a great example of mutualism.

The rhino and tickbird have other ways of helping each other out. As the tickbird rides on the rhino's back, it can see lots of things the rhino can't, such as a predator coming closer. The tickbird warns the rhino by making lots of noise when a predator is near. In return, riding on top of a rhino gives the bird a safe home with plenty to eat. Rhinos can grow to about fourteen feet long and six feet tall, so many animals don't want to mess with them. The small tickbird is protected by the rhino's huge size. As the large rhino runs, it kicks up clouds of dust and insects. The tickbird eats these insects as well as the ticks on the rhino's back. All in all, the tickbird and rhino have a win-win living arrangement.

The rhino gives us a good example of both parasitism and mutualism. While ticks feed off the rhino and cause him harm, the tickbird eats the ticks and helps the rhino out. These animals show us two different types of symbiosis, or living together. Having a roommate can be difficult, but if you practice mutualism, everybody wins.

**Fill in the Venn Diagram to show the similarities
and differences between parasitism and mutualism.**

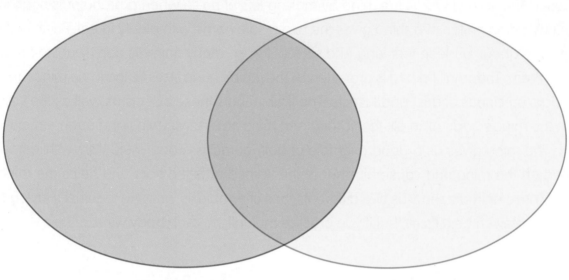

Parasitism

Mutualism

Circle the conclusions that are logical and could be supported with facts from the passage.

Ticks and tickbirds have a relationship of mutualism.

Without tickbirds, rhinos would have lots of ticks on their backs.

Rhinos, ticks, and tickbirds live in the same habitat.

Tickbirds and rhinos make better roommates than ticks and rhinos.

Rhinos do not spend a lot of time in the grass.

List some facts that support the conclusion below.

Conclusion: Rhinos and tickbirds need each other.

Support:

_____

_____

_____

_____

_____

_____

_____

Battle of the School Bands

Last Friday the Battle of the School Bands concert filled the auditorium with music and energy. Bands from three elementary schools gathered to play their best songs and compete for the title of Best School Band. As each band took the stage, they played three different songs in the hopes of impressing the audience. Now that all three bands have performed, students have the chance to vote on which band deserves the title of Best Band. I think that all the bands did a good job, but one stands out as the best.

Holton Elementary was the first school band to perform. The band players looked very sharp and professional in their matching black shirts. The band not only looked unified, they sounded unified as well! They played three upbeat jazz songs that had many people snapping right along. The saxophone and clarinet players did a great job of carrying the jazzy melody. The teachers in the audience especially enjoyed the numbers and seemed to recognize some of the songs. It was clear that the band had worked hard to prepare such a great performance.

I liked Holton's well-played jazz songs, but the performance sometimes lacked energy. It seemed the players were so concerned about getting all the notes right, they forgot to have fun. This band needs to work on relaxing and enjoying the music more.

Mapleleaf School was next to take the stage. Every year they have a great drum section, and this year was no exception. The drums kept the beat going strong on every song. The first two numbers were rock and roll songs, and the band even had singers. Both of the songs had long drum solos that made the audience go wild. Their final number was an African song with lots of drums and a unique melody.

Mapleleaf's band had many strengths, and their African song was a highlight of the show. The drummers' solos were especially great. However, I disagreed with the band's choice to include singers in the performance. The singers distracted from the band's playing and made it difficult to hear the music.

Lynnfield Elementary was the final band to perform, and they played three very different songs. They started with a slow, classical song that pleased everyone. The student sitting next to me whispered, "That was great, and I don't even like classical music!" Next, they surprised everyone by playing a country song! They even had a few banjo and harmonica players. We couldn't help but stand up, clap our hands, and dance along. The Lynnfield band ended their performance with a folk song. The upbeat melody seemed to float over the audience, and both students and teachers were singing along. The band members gave off so much energy and looked like they really enjoyed playing.

I feel that Lynnfield did the best job because their songs showed the most range. The band proved they could play all different types of music and have fun while doing it. They did the best job of capturing the whole audience's attention, and they deserve to be named Best School Band!

The final winner will be announced this Friday. Audience members need to turn in their votes and comments to the judges by Wednesday night. Hopefully, Lynnfield's band will be receiving the trophy for their amazing performance!

Use the words in the box to complete the outline.

three	Mapleleaf	African	folk
vote	jazz	classical	range
unified	drum	country	audience

I. Introduction

  a) 1) _____ elementary schools competed in Battle of the Bands

  b) Students can 2) _____ on the best band

II. Holton School

  a) Looked and sounded 3) _____

  b) Played three 4) _____ songs

  c) Enjoyed by teachers

  d) Lacked energy

III. 5) _____ School

  a) Strong 6) _____ section and solos

  b) Played two rock songs with singers

  d) Closed with a unique 7) _____ song

  e) Singers distracted from the band

IV. Lynnfield School

  a) Started with a slow 8) _____ song

  b) Played a 9) _____ song with banjos and harmonicas

  c) Closed with a 10) _____ song

  d) Lots of energy and fun

  e) Showed the most 11) _____

  f) Captured the whole 12) _____

Answer the questions.

1. The audience for this passage is _____.
   a) students who might vote on the Battle of the School Bands concert
   b) musicians who like African music
   c) teachers who want to compete in the Battle of the School Bands

2. The purpose of this passage is to _____.
   a) convince people to go to the Battle of the School Bands concert
   b) describe the concert and argue that Lynnfield did the best
   c) persuade students to vote for Holton Elementary School

3. The tone of this passage is _____.
   a) angry
   b) humorous
   c) persuasive

4. The writer quotes another student in the audience to _____.
   a) reinforce his point that the classical song was good
   b) point out that most kids don't like jazz
   c) persuade the audience to listen to more country music

5. Summarize why the writer feels that Lynnfield's band is the best.

   _____

   _____

   _____

   _____

   _____

   _____

   _____

   _____

   _____

   _____

Pass It On

Sarah felt the car's engine sputter and shake as it inched up the mountain. As her father steered the car to the shoulder of the road, they coasted to a slow stop. They had gotten lost on their way to the ski slopes, and now they were out of gas.

A few minutes later, a car pulled over beside them. The driver rolled down her window and asked if she could help. When Sarah's dad explained that they were out of gas, the woman popped her trunk and got out a silver can.

"There's enough gas in this can to get you to the next gas station," the woman explained. She also gave Sarah's dad a map and told him how to get to the slopes.

As Sarah's dad poured the gas into his tank, the woman waved goodbye and drove away.

"You forgot your can!" he shouted, but it was too late. So he put the empty can in the back seat with Sarah.

"Hey look," Sarah said, "the words 'Pass it on' are written on the gas can" she said. "What do you think it means?"

"I think it means that we should pass the can on to the next person in need," her mother said.

When they filled up their car at the gas station, they also filled up the gas can. Sarah watched for people who might need their help as they drove up the mountain.

They pulled up behind a white sports car that was going very slowly.

"If we stay behind this slow car we'll never get to the slopes!" Sarah said.

Then the white car pulled off the road.

"They're probably out of gas. We should help," Sarah's dad said.

They slowly turned around and drove back to the white car. Sarah noticed that a mother and her young daughter were in the car. She knew she was doing the right thing as she handed them the gas can.

"Thank you so much!" the woman said.

"It's no problem," Sarah said as she smiled. "Just pass it on!"

Draw arrows to show how each event led to the next.

Sarah's car ran out of gas on their way up the mountain.

A woman gave them a gas can and drove away before they could return it.

Sarah saw the words "Pass it on" written on the can.

Sarah's dad refilled the can with gas.

Sarah passed the can on to another person in need.

Answer the questions.

1. How did the woman help Sarah's family? _____
   _____

2. Why did the woman drive away without getting her can back?_____
   _____

3. Why did the people in the white car need help?_____
   _____

4. How did Sarah feel when she passed the can on?_____
   _____
   _____

5. Circle the sentence that best expresses the story's theme.
   a) Driving up a mountain is dangerous.
   b) If you're prepared, you'll never run out of gas.
   c) If someone is generous to you, pass the kindness on.

Movie Review

Learning to become a good writer will help your reading comprehension skills. Write a review of the most recent movie you saw. Answer the questions below to brainstorm ideas. Then write your review on the next page.

Movie title:

_____

Summary of the plot:

_____

_____

_____

_____

_____

Favorite parts:

_____

_____

_____

Least favorite parts:

_____

_____

_____

Would you recommend this movie? Why or why not?

_____

_____

_____

How could the movie have been better?

_____

_____

Write your movie review on the lines below.

Remember, a review not only summarizes what happened,

it gives opinions about the strengths and weaknesses too!

_____

_____

_____

_____

_____

_____

_____

_____

_____

_____

_____

_____

_____

_____

_____

_____

_____

_____

_____

_____

_____

_____

_____

_____

Answer Key

Page 6
Top of page
1. d   2. e
3. a   4. b
5. c
Bottom of page
1. alpine
2. snowline
3. photosynthesis
4. scorch
5. withstand
6. devoted
7. noble
8. endangered

Page 7
Answers will vary.
1. The alpine biome is at a high altitude, so the air is thin and the sun is intense. The soil is dry and rocky. It's cold and windy, so there are no tall trees.
2. 200
3. At high elevations there is less oxygen, making photosynthesis more difficult.
4. Alpine plants stay close to the ground because it is so cold and windy that anything tall would blow over.
5. The plant's deep roots and thick leaves help it survive.
6. Reaching an edelweiss plant was dangerous, so young men picked them to prove their courage and love.
7. Edelweiss does not re-grow easily, so the plant is endangered.
8. The edelweiss plant has features that help it survive in the harsh alpine biome.

Page 10

	Snuba	Scuba
1. Where is the air tank?	On a raft on the water's surface.	On the diver's back.
2. How deep can the diver go?	20 feet.	Hundreds of feet.
3. Describe the equipment.	A mask, harness, weight belt, mouthpiece	A mask, air tanks, wet suit, weights
4. How much training is needed?	A few minutes	You must take classes and be certified.
5. What's the minimum age?	4	15

Snuba and scuba both allow a person to stay underwater for an extended period of time. They both allow the swimmer to explore the underwater world. They both use a mask and air tanks to "breathe" underwater.

Page 11
Logical Conclusions:
Scuba diving is more dangerous than snuba.
Learning how to scuba takes more time and money than learning snuba.
Snuba and scuba are both great ways to see the underwater world.
Conclusion: For a family with young children, snuba is a better activity than scuba.
Support: Snuba can be done by kids as young as 4, while you must be 15 to scuba.
Snuba can be learned quickly and does not involve heavy gear.

Page 14
1. facts   2. bicycle
3. foot   4. Motorized
5. engine   6. illegal
7. sidewalk   8. highways
9. lights   10. himself
11. private   12. sixteen
13. license   14. fined
15. Safety

Page 15
Answer the questions.
1. a   2. c
3. b   4. a
5. Motorized scooters are dangerous and kids shouldn't ride them.

Page 17
Laura learned about earthquakes in school.
↓
Laura worried about earthquakes a lot.
↓
She earthquake-proofed the house and made her family do drills.
↓
One night the family heard a loud rumbling.
↓
Laura realized she was prepared and didn't need to be afraid.
1. At first she was so worried she wanted to do drills all the time. Then she realized she was prepared and she felt more relaxed.
2. They earthquake-proofed the house by bolting all the shelves, putting latches on the cabinets, and rearranging furniture. They also did earthquake drills.
3. Laura felt calm, but Byron panicked and felt afraid.
4. Answers will vary.
5. a

Page 20
Top of page
1. a   2. c   3. e
4. d   5. b
Bottom of page
1. afterlife
2. embalmer
3. organs
4. shrouds
5. mummify
6. coffin
7. tomb
8. burial

Page 21
Answers may vary.
1. They believed their body and soul would be reunited in the afterlife, but the journey to the afterlife was dangerous.
2. The eyes were for the person in the coffin to see into the living world.
3. The more mourners at the funeral, the more important the person was.
4. Wealthy people had pyramids for tombs. Tombs were also carved out of cliffs and built underground.
5. They believed that the shabti statues would come to life and be servants.
6. They found food, jewelry, games, and even a couch.
7. The coffin decorations and items in the tomb show us about Egyptian beliefs.
8. 5, 4, 3, 1, 2, 6

Page 24
Answers will vary.
inside the left circle
2 days admission
50 ride coupons
Live music show
Some money gets donated back to schools
Must be purchased at an Elementary school before the fair
Costs $10.00 for adults and $5.00 for kids
Positive comments from parents and kids
inside the middle circle
Petting zoo admission
Unlimited hot dog and drinks
Must be purchased in advance
inside right circle
1 day admission
Unlimited rides
Magic show
Front row seats at pig races

Can be purchased at Pinewood businesses
Costs $20.00 for adults or children

Page 25
Logical Conclusions:
The Fair Fun Wristband is more expensive than the Pinewood Pass.
You cannot buy the wristband or the pass at the fair.
If you like live music more than magic, you should buy the Pinewood Pass.
Conclusion: Many parents in Pinewood support the Pinewood Pass.
Support: Money from the Pinewood Pass goes back to Pinewood schools.
Two Pinewood parents said they liked the Pinewood Pass.
The pass is approved by the Pinewood Parents Association.

Page 28
1. solar
2. panels
3. cardboard box
4. collect
5. parabola
6. poster board
7. tin foil
8. focal point
9. roasting
10. renewable

Page 29
1. c   2. b
3. c   4. b
5. Cut a parabolic curve in the top of a cardboard box. Cover the top with poster board and then glue tin foil to the poster board. Tape cardboard to the sides of the box and push a skewer through. Roast your hot dog right above the focal point.

Page 31
Top of page
1. c   2. b   3. a
Bottom of Page
1. Kristine is visiting her friend Keikko in Japan.
2. Flower Festival
3. They wear kimonos, march in a parade with flowers, visit the Buddhist temple, and write messages on lanterns.
4. Kristine wishes to always remember the festival.
5. c

Answer Key

Page 34

Top of page

1. e   2. c   3. d
4. a   5. b

Bottom of page

1. Babylonia   2. Code
3. columns   4. crimes
5. punishment   6. instructions
7. quality   8. justice

Page 35

Answers may vary.

1. It was the first set of detailed laws put in writing.
2. Cuneiform is the writing system used in ancient Mesopotamia. It has over 2,000 symbols, compared to 64 English symbols.
3. He named all the city-states in his empire and explained that the Code was to ensure people would get justice.
4. Owning property was very important to people during this time.
5. "Eye for an eye" meant that the punishment should be equal to the crime. If a man broke someone's bones, his own bones would be broken in return.
6. The laws were carved into stone so they would be unchangeable. People use the phrase "written in stone" to mean that something is final.
7. They make sure that everyone is treated the same way.
8. Hammarabi's Code, the first set of detailed written laws, described rules and punishments about stealing, business, farming, and family life in ancient Mesopotamia.

Page 38

1. Sparta: Education focused on physical strength and toughness.
   Athens: Boys learned reading, writing, math, music, poetry, and drama.
2. Sparta: All men served in the military until they were 60.
   Athens: Boys 18 to 20 served for 2 years.
3. Sparta: Girls were given some physical training to be tough.
   Athens: Girls were expected to stay indoors.
4. Sparta: They had an Assembly and two kings, but a group of five men had the real power.

Athens: They elected Assembly leaders every year and voted on laws.
5. Sparta: They liked independence and left other cities alone.
   Athens: They wanted to conquer other lands.

Bottom of page:

They shared the same language, religion, and customs. Spartans and Athenians were both proud of their Greek identity. Both city-states required some military service from their men. They also both had an Assembly of lawmakers.

Page 39

Logical Conclusions:

Sparta had a stronger army than Athens.
Athenians had a more balanced education than Spartans.
Art, music, and poetry were not important to Spartans.
Conclusion: Athenians were more creative than Spartans.
Support: Poetry and drama were important in Athens, but not in Sparta.
Spartans did not teach boys how to read, write, or practice the arts.
Athenian boys were taught music and the arts were encouraged.
Athenians enjoyed debating issues and exchanging ideas.

Page 42

1. meteors   2. rice
3. ice   4. tail
5. dust   6. gravity
7. atmosphere   8. shower
9. August   10. Perseus
11. telescope   12. midnight

Page 43

1. b   2. c
3. a   4. b
5. Comets leave behind a tail of dust particles. The particles explode when they hit the Earth's atmosphere. Each burning speck of comet dust makes a flash of light in the sky.

Page 45

Top of page

1. c   2. a   3. b

Bottom of page

1. Bruno found Anthony at the souvenir stand.
2. The four teams were red, white, blue, and green.
3. They wrapped the reins

around their waists.
4. The trumpeter played and the emperor gave Diocles a palm branch and wreath of laurel leaves.
5. b

Page 48

Top of page

1. e   2. d   3. c
4. a   5. b

Bottom of page

1. lightweight   2. rubber
3. Goodyear   4. flexible
5. creepers   6. recreation
7. teenagers   8. casual

Page 49

Answers may vary.

1. Goodyear couldn't get the rubber to stick to the canvas.
2. Goodyear discovered that heat made rubber strong and flexible.
3. They were called gumshoes because of the elastic rubber sole.
4. The shoes were very quiet and didn't make noise.
5. Basketball player Chuck Taylor's name was printed on a popular pair of sneakers.
6. Converse All Stars
7. Teenagers wore sneakers to express themselves.
8. Sneakers started out as a lightweight shoe for sports like tennis. They got their name because the rubber sole made them very quiet. Sneakers grew in popularity and more styles developed.

Page 52

Answers will vary.

inside the left circle

The parasite benefits, but the other animal is harmed.
A tick is a parasite on a rhino.
The tick sucks the rhino's blood and spreads disease.

inside the middle circle

Symbiosis
Two animals living together

inside the right circle

Both animals benefit
The tick bird gets a meal and the rhino gets rid of ticks.
The tick bird and the rhino protect each other.

Page 53

Logical Conclusions:

Tickbirds and rhinos make better roommates than ticks and rhinos.

rhinos, ticks, and tickbirds live in the same habitat.
Without tickbirds, rhinos would have lots of ticks on their backs.
Conclusion: Rhinos and tickbirds need each other.
Support: Rhinos need to get rid of the ticks, and tickbirds need food. Tickbirds get protection from riding on top of the rhino. Tickbirds make noise when a predator is near, which protects the rhino.

Page 56

1. Three   2. vote
3. unified   4. jazz
5. Mapleleaf   6. drum
7. African   8. classical
9. country   10. folk
11. range   12. audience

Page 57

1. a   2. b
3. c   4. a
5. The writer felt that Lynnfield's band showed the most range, had fun while they were playing, and captured the audience's attention the best.

Page 59

Sarah's car ran out of gas on their way up the mountain.
↓
A woman gave them a gas can and drove away before they could return it.
↓
Sarah saw the words "Pass it on" written on the can.
↓
Sarah's dad refilled the can with gas.
↓
Sarah passed the can on to another person in need.

1. The woman gave them gas and a map.
2. She wanted Sarah's family to keep the can and pass it on.
3. The car was out of gas.
4. She felt good that she had helped someone else.
5. c

Page 60

Answers will vary.

Page 61

Answers will vary.

Nice work!

_____,
(Name)

you're a
reading
champion!

READING
CHAMPION